CHRISTIANITY E✝PLORED

Christianity Explored is written by Rico Tice, Barry Cooper and Sam Shammas.

Copyright © 2003 Rico Tice

First published in 2001.
2nd Edition published in 2003. Reprinted 2003 (twice), 2004 (twice), 2005 (twice).
This 2007 version of the 2nd Edition, reprinted 2007, 2008, 2009 (twice), 2010.

Published by:
The Good Book Company Ltd
Elm House, 37 Elm Road, New Malden, Surrey KT3 3HB, UK
Tel: +44 (0)845 225 0880; Fax: +44 (0)845 225 0990
email: admin@thegoodbook.co.uk

websites:
UK: www.thegoodbook.co.uk
N America: www.thegoodbook.com
Australia: www.thegoodbook.com.au
New Zealand: www.thegoodbook.co.nz

The right of Rico Tice to be identified as the author of this work has been asserted by him in accordance with the Copyright, Designs and Patents Act 1988.

ISBN: 9781904889335
Designed by Diane Bainbridge
Printed in China. ICTI no C2446

CHRISTIANITY E✝PLORED

STUDY GUIDE

CONTENTS

PREFACE
BEFORE WE BEGIN

THE JOURNEY AHEAD

Welcome to *Christianity Explored*.

Over the next ten weeks, we will explore three questions that cut right to the heart of Christianity: Who was Jesus? Why did he come? What is involved in following him?

Don't be afraid to ask questions, no matter how simple or difficult you think they are. And if you have to miss a week, don't worry. You can always ask someone in your group for a quick summary of what you've missed.

So who was Jesus? Why did he come? And what does it mean to follow him?

OUR GUIDE, MARK

To help us answer those questions, we're going to use one of the books of the Bible. It's a book named after its author, Mark.

But before we start looking at the Bible, here are some tips on finding your way around it:

- The Bible is divided into two main sections: the Old Testament and the New Testament. The Old Testament was written before Jesus was born and the New Testament was written after Jesus was born.

- There are 66 books in the Bible: 39 in the Old Testament and 27 in the New Testament.

- Every Bible has a contents page at the front that will help you find the books referred to in this *Study Guide*.

- Each book of the Bible is divided up into chapters and each chapter is further divided into individual verses, all of which are numbered.

So "Mark 1:1 – 3:6" refers to the book of Mark, chapter 1, verse 1, through to chapter 3, verse 6. All the Bible references in this *Study Guide* are written in this way.

- There are four accounts of Jesus' life in the Bible, all named after their authors: Matthew, Mark, Luke and John. They're known as "Gospels" (the word "gospel" literally means "good news").

- You can find the book of Mark (also known as Mark's Gospel) about three-quarters of the way through your Bible, between the books of Matthew and Luke.

WHY SHOULD WE READ MARK'S GOSPEL?

One reason to read Mark is that his book is the shortest of the four Gospels!

Another reason is that Mark opens his book with a staggering claim. In his first sentence, Mark claims that Jesus Christ is "the Son of God" (Mark 1:1). In other words, Mark tells us that Jesus is God in human form.

By reading Mark, you have the opportunity to prove – or disprove – the writer's claim.

CAN WE RELY ON MARK'S GOSPEL?

You may be wondering whether Mark is a reliable place to find out about Jesus. So it's important to ask the same questions we should ask of any document that claims to record history:

What do we know about the author?
Mark was a close associate of Peter, who was one of Jesus' "apostles" (those who Jesus specifically called to be witnesses of his life; see Mark 3:14). Papias, writing in about AD 130, recorded the connection between Mark and Peter: "Mark being the interpreter of Peter, whatsoever he recorded he wrote with great accuracy."

When was the document written?
Peter clearly knew he would soon be killed for his belief in Jesus and wrote: "I will make every effort to see that after my departure you will always be

able to remember these things" (2 Peter 1:15). Peter died in the mid-sixties AD, so the evidence suggests that Mark wrote his Gospel either just before or just after Peter's death, in order to accurately preserve Peter's eyewitness testimony.

Was it written a long time after the events it records?

Jesus died in about AD 30. That means there was a gap of around thirty years between the events Mark records and the date he wrote about them. This is well within the lifetime of those who lived through the events he describes, so many of Mark's readers would have been able to spot any fabrications or inconsistencies. There were also many hostile eyewitnesses who were anxious to discredit him. Mark had to make sure that his account was trustworthy.

Have the original documents been accurately passed down to us?

If the originals of the Bible or any other ancient document do not exist, then the following questions need to be asked to assess the reliability of the copies:

- how old are the copies?
- how much time has elapsed between the composition of the original document and the copies that now exist?
- how many copies have been found?

> *The table below answers these questions for three widely trusted historical works and compares them with the New Testament. Fill in the blank space, and compare your guess with the answer at the bottom of the page.*

	Date of original document	Date of oldest surviving copy	Approximate time between original and oldest surviving copy	Number of ancient copies in existence today
THUCYDIDES' HISTORY OF THE PELOPONNESIAN WAR	c. 431–400 BC	AD 900 plus a few late 1st century fragments	1,300 years	73
CAESAR'S GALLIC WAR	c. 58–50 BC	AD 825	875 years	10
TACITUS' HISTORIES AND ANNALS	c. AD 98–108	c. AD 850	750 years	2
THE NEW TESTAMENT	AD 40–100 (Mark AD 60–65)	AD 350 (Mark 3rd century)	310 years	*

*14,000 (approximately 5,000 Greek; 8,000 Latin; and 1,000 in other languages)

As the table shows, the interval between the original composition date of the New Testament and the date of the oldest surviving copy is comparatively small. Moreover, in contrast to the other works, there are an enormous number of early manuscript copies or portions of the New Testament.

Do other historical documents support Mark's account of Jesus?

Even without the New Testament accounts of Jesus or other Christian writings we still have plenty of evidence concerning the life and claims of Jesus. For example, the Samaritan historian Thallus (AD 52) discusses the darkness that fell during the crucifixion (recorded in Mark 15:33). And Josephus, a Jewish historian writing in the first century AD, has the following to say: "Now there was about this time Jesus, a wise man, if it be lawful to call him a man; for he was a doer of wonderful works, a teacher of such men as receive the truth with pleasure. He drew over to him both many of the Jews, and many of the Gentiles. He was [the] Christ. And when Pilate, at the suggestion of the principal men among us, had condemned him to the cross, those that loved him at the first did not forsake him; for he appeared to them alive again the third day; as the divine prophets had foretold these and ten thousand other wonderful things concerning him. And the tribe of the Christians, so named from him, are not extinct at this day."

EXPLORING MARK'S GOSPEL

Each week, you'll have the opportunity to explore a few chapters of Mark.

The HOME STUDY sections provide questions to help you do this. By the end of Week 6, you'll have read through the whole of Mark's Gospel.

As a group you'll also look in detail at passages of particular interest.

Here are some tips to help you get the most out of Mark's Gospel:

• Remember that Mark is writing with a clear purpose: to tell people the good news about Jesus (Mark 1:1). Mark's Gospel is not just a random collection of incidents from Jesus' life and extracts from his teaching. Instead, he carefully selects events from the life of Jesus, and deliberately places them in a certain order. He does this because he wants his readers to understand exactly who Jesus was.

A good example of this occurs in Mark 15:33–39. Why does Mark take us from events at the cross outside the city walls of Jerusalem (verses 33–37), to the temple in the heart of the city (verse 38), and then back to the cross (verse 39)? It's because he wants us to understand that these events are connected in some way and tell us something about Jesus.

- As with any book, context is very important. If you come across something you don't understand, ask yourself what has happened immediately before, and take into account what happens immediately afterwards.

- It's also important to set Mark in the context of the Bible as a whole. Just as it would make no sense to start reading Mark's Gospel at chapter 10 without thinking about what he has written in the first nine chapters, it's also vital to see how Mark fits in to the overall narrative of the Bible. Throughout the Old Testament, we read of God's gradually unfolding plan to draw people into a relationship with him. In Mark's Gospel, we see that plan reaching its conclusion. The Old Testament quotations in Mark help us to understand this.

For example, in Mark 1:2–3, Mark quotes from the Old Testament. Why does he do that? And why does he do it at this point? It's because he wants us to understand that the events he describes are part of a bigger picture.

As you explore Mark's Gospel, you will be able to discover for yourself who Jesus was, why he came, and what it would mean to follow him.

WEEK 1
INTRODUCTION

GROUP DISCUSSION 1

Welcome to *Christianity Explored*.

TALK OUTLINE

"The beginning of the gospel about Jesus Christ, the Son of God."
(Mark 1:1)

- There are many reasons to suspect that God might exist: the order of the universe, the beauty of the world and the incredible design of the human body. There's also the nagging sense that nothing we do or achieve will fully satisfy us, that something is missing in life.

- But how can we know for sure that God exists? We would need him to introduce himself. And according to Mark, that's exactly what God has done. In order to introduce himself to us, he has become a man: the person we call Jesus Christ.

- Christianity is about being able to have a relationship with God. That's why "the gospel about Jesus Christ" is good news.

NOTES

- If you could ask God one question, and you knew it would be answered, what would it be?

- What is *your* view of Christianity?

- How do you feel about making time to read Mark?

HOME STUDY

Each week you'll be exploring a few chapters of Mark. By the end of Week 6, you'll have read the whole of Mark's Gospel.

> *Read Mark 1:1 – 3:6.*

Summary: Jesus' true identity begins to emerge, but the religious authorities oppose him.

> *Use the following study to help you explore the passage. There's room at the end for you to write down any questions you'd like to discuss next time.*

1 **In Mark 1:1–13, who points to Jesus?**
  (look in particular at verses 2, 7 and 11)

2 **Who is Jesus said to be in these verses?**

3 **What sort of power and authority does Jesus exercise?**
  (see Mark 1:16–20, 21–22, 23–28, 40–45; 2:1–12)

continued »

4 What has Jesus come to do? (see Mark 1:14–15, 35–39; 2:17)

5 Notice that Jesus' priority is preaching – it comes before healing the body. Why might that be?

6 Who opposes Jesus and why do you think this might be? (see Mark 2:6–7, 16; 3:2–6)

7 What do the opening chapters of Mark tell you about who Jesus is? What are the implications for how you relate to Jesus?

Your questions on this HOME STUDY

WEEK 2
JESUS - WHO WAS HE?

GROUP DISCUSSION 1

> Discuss any questions arising from last week's HOME STUDY.

> Look together at Mark 2:1–12 and answer the questions below:

1 The passage opens by telling us that so many people had gathered to hear Jesus that there was no room left. Why had so many people come to hear Jesus?
(look at Mark 1:27–28, 32–34, 45 for clues)

2 Why did these people bring their friend to Jesus?

3 In view of the situation, what is surprising about what Jesus says in Mark 2:5?

4 Why were the teachers of the law so annoyed about Jesus'
remark? (see Mark 2:6–7)

5 Were they right?

6 How do we know that Jesus has authority to forgive sin?
(see Mark 2:8–12)

7 What does this incident imply about who Jesus is?
(see Mark 2:7)

8 Why do you think Jesus said, "Son, your sins are forgiven"
before healing the man?

TALK OUTLINE

"Who is this? Even the wind and the waves obey him!" (Mark 4:41)

- It's important to get Jesus' identity right – otherwise we'll relate to him in the wrong way.

NOTES

- Mark presents us with five blocks of evidence, five different areas in which Jesus demonstrated the power and authority of God.

- Jesus demonstrated power and authority:

  - to teach (Mark 1:21–22)

  - over sickness (Mark 1:29–31)

  - over nature (Mark 4:35–41)

  - over death (Mark 5:35–42)

  - to forgive sins (Mark 2:1–12)

- **What is your view of Jesus?**

- **What do you think of the five blocks of evidence Mark gives us?**

HOME STUDY

> *Read Mark 3:7 – 5:43.*

Summary: Jesus' identity continues to emerge as he teaches and displays miraculous power.

> *Use the following study to help you explore the passage. There's room at the end for you to write down any questions you'd like to discuss next time.*

1 **What does Jesus exercise power and authority over?**
   (see Mark 4:35–41; 5:1–20, 25–34, 35–43)

2 What does this add to what we saw of Jesus' power and authority in Mark 1:1 – 3:6?

3 What is the disciples' concern in Mark 4:38? What is Jesus' assessment of them in Mark 4:40?

4 Describe the situation of the woman in Mark 5:25–26. What happens to her in Mark 5:27–29? What is Jesus' assessment of her in Mark 5:34?

5 Describe the situation of Jairus in Mark 5:35. What is Jesus' assessment of him in Mark 5:36?

6 What do these incidents teach us about who Jesus is?

continued »

7 What are the different ways in which people respond to Jesus? (see Mark 4:40–41; 5:15, 34, 36)

8 Which of these responses to Jesus do you most relate to?

Your questions on this HOME STUDY

WEEK 3
JESUS - WHY DID HE COME?

GROUP DISCUSSION 1

▷ *Discuss any questions arising from last week's HOME STUDY.*

▷ *Look together at Mark 4:35–41 and answer the questions below:*

1 Why are the disciples afraid in Mark 4:37–38?

2 What is so remarkable about the way in which Jesus calms the storm? (see Mark 4:39)

3 What is surprising about Jesus' response to the disciples? (see Mark 4:40)

4 Why don't the disciples have faith – in other words, why don't they trust Jesus? (see Mark 4:41)

5 What should the disciples have understood from this incident, bearing in mind they were Jews who would have been steeped in the Old Testament?
(see Psalms 89:9; 65:5–7; 107:23–30)

6 How would *you* answer the disciples' question in Mark 4:41 – "Who is this? Even the wind and the waves obey him!"

TALK OUTLINE

"I have not come to call the righteous, but sinners." (Mark 2:17)

- The reason that the world is not as it should be is because we are not as we should be.

- When asked what the greatest commandment was, Jesus replied, "Love the Lord your God with all your heart and with all your soul and with all your mind and with all your strength" (Mark 12:30). But none of us have lived like that.

- We've all rebelled against God, and the Bible calls this "sin."

- Jesus tells us that "sin" comes "from within," from our "hearts" (Mark 7:20–22).

- This means that we're all in danger, whether we realize it or not (Mark 9:43–47).

- Jesus came to rescue us from our sin.

NOTES

• **Do you agree that you're in danger?**

• **How would you feel if your every thought, word and action was displayed on the walls for everyone to see?**

• **What's your reaction to Jesus' words in Mark chapter 9, verses 43–47?**

HOME STUDY

▷ *Read Mark 6:1 – 8:29.*

Summary: Despite the amazement that Jesus continues to generate, many reject him. Jesus explains why.

▷ *Use the following study to help you explore the passage. There's room at the end for you to write down any questions you'd like to discuss next time.*

1 **What does this passage add to what we've seen of Jesus' power and authority in chapters 1–5? (see Mark 6:32–44, 47–48; 7:31–37; 8:1–10, 22–26)**

2 **How are people responding to Jesus as they see his power and authority? (see Mark 6:1–6, 14–16, 51–56; 7:37; 8:11)**

3 **According to Jesus, what is the real need of the people? (see Mark 6:34; 7:14–23)**

4 **In view of all that Jesus has said and done, what is so surprising about the disciples' response? (see Mark 6:35–37, 51; 7:17–18; 8:4, 14–21)**

continued »

5 Now that you're halfway through Mark's Gospel, and have read about the amazing things that Jesus said and did, how would you answer Jesus' question in Mark 8:29?

Your questions on this HOME STUDY

WEEK 4
JESUS - HIS DEATH

GROUP DISCUSSION 1

> Discuss any questions arising from last week's HOME STUDY.

> Look together at Mark 8:17–29 and answer the questions below:

1 **Generally speaking, who do people today believe Jesus to be? On what do they base their views?**

2 **How does Jesus describe the disciples in Mark 8:17, 18 and 21?**

3 "Do you still not understand?" What should the disciples have understood? (see Mark 8:17–21; see also Exodus 16:11–15, where God miraculously feeds people in the desert)

4 What happens in Mark 8:29, and why is this important?

5 Why do you think Mark describes a miracle (the healing of the blind man) between Mark 8:21 and Mark 8:29? How have the disciples come to understand who Jesus is?

6 In Mark 8:29, Jesus asks: "But what about you? Who do you say I am?" How would you answer and why?

TALK OUTLINE

"For even the Son of Man did not come to be served, but to serve, and to give his life as a ransom for many." (Mark 10:45)

- Jesus went to his death willingly and quite deliberately. In fact, he knew it was necessary.

- As Jesus died on the cross, the darkness that fell was a sign of God's anger and judgement. And Jesus' cry – "My God, my God, why have you forsaken me?" (Mark 15:34) – shows that Jesus was abandoned by God.

- He was abandoned so that we need never be. He died taking the anger and judgement that our sin deserves. God was sacrificing himself by sending his Son to die in our place.

- As Jesus died, the curtain in the temple was torn in two from top to bottom. This illustrates the fact that Jesus' death opens the way for sinful people to come into God's presence.

- Mark records the reactions of those who witness Jesus' death:

  - the busy soldiers (Mark 15:24)
  - the self-satisfied religious leaders (Mark 15:31–32)
  - the cowardly Pontius Pilate (Mark 15:15)
  - the detached bystander (Mark 15:35–36)
  - the Roman centurion, who recognized that Jesus was "the Son of God" (Mark 15:39)

NOTES

- **Can you identify with any of the reactions to Jesus' death on the cross?**

- **Jesus said he came "to give his life as a ransom for many" (Mark 10:45). How do you feel about that?**

HOME STUDY

> *Read Mark 8:30 – 10:52.*

Summary: Jesus predicts his own death in detail, and teaches his followers what it will mean for them.

> *Use the following study to help you explore the passage. There's room at the end for you to write down any questions you'd like to discuss next time.*

1 Jesus predicts his own death three times. What does he say "must" and "will" happen? (see Mark 8:31, 9:31 and 10:33–34. Note that "Son of Man" is Jesus' way of referring to himself.)

2 Why must Jesus die? (see Mark 10:45)

3 Three times Jesus predicts his own death and Mark records the disciples' response each time. How do the disciples respond and why? (see Mark 8:32–33; 9:33–35; 10:35–45)

4 What has Jesus taught the disciples that following him will mean? (see Mark 8:34)

continued »

5 Peter sees that Jesus is the Christ (that is, God's anointed King), but he doesn't yet behave as if that were true (see Mark 8:32). How should he have behaved? How should *you* behave towards Jesus?

Your questions on this HOME STUDY

WEEK 5
WHAT IS GRACE?

GROUP DISCUSSION 1

> Discuss any questions arising from last week's HOME STUDY.

> Look together at Mark 10:17–22 and answer the questions below:

1 What do we learn about the man and his attitude to Jesus in Mark 10:17?

2 What should the man have understood about himself from what Jesus says in Mark 10:18? And how should he have reacted?

3 What did Jesus expect the man to notice about his list of the
   commandments in Mark 10:19? (compare what Jesus says
   with the list of commandments in Deuteronomy 5:6–21)

4 So, what should the man have understood about himself
   from what Jesus says in Mark 10:19? Again, how should he
   have reacted?

5 How does Jesus expose the man's failure to keep the first
   commandment? (see Deuteronomy 5:7 and Mark 10:21–22)

6 Where does the man place his confidence – with wealth or
   with God? Where do you place *your* confidence?

"For it is by grace you have been saved, through faith – and this not from yourselves, it is the gift of God – not by works, so that no-one can boast." (Ephesians 2:8–9)

- We can't make ourselves acceptable to God by doing "good things." These things may be wonderful in themselves, but they can't solve the problem of our sin.

- We are only acceptable to God because of Jesus' death. When we look at what happened at the cross, we see God freely offering us forgiveness.

- This is something we cannot earn and do not deserve. And that's grace: God behaving toward us in a way we simply do not deserve.

- We don't have to pretend to be something we're not. We don't have to be constantly proving ourselves to God. God's love for us is unconditional.

NOTES

WEEK 5

- If you were in the bishop's place, would you have given Valjean the candlesticks as well?

- Has grace made a difference to your view of God?

- What do people generally do to be accepted by God, if they bother at all?

HOME STUDY

> *Read Mark 11:1 – 13:37.*

Summary: Jesus goes to Jerusalem, and comes into confrontation with the religious authorities.

> *Use the following study to help you explore the passage. There's room at the end for you to write down any questions you'd like to discuss next time.*

1 What is the crowd's attitude towards Jesus as he arrives in Jerusalem? (see Mark 11:8–10)

2 What is the religious authorities' attitude to Jesus in Mark 11:18 and Mark 12:12?

3 As a result of this attitude, how do they treat Jesus? (see Mark 11:27–33; 12:13–17, 18–27)

4 The religious authorities are steeped in the Old Testament and Jesus knows how familiar they are with it (in Mark 11:17 he says, "Is it not written..." and in Mark 12:10, "Haven't you read this scripture..."). What is the significance of the detail in Mark 11:1–10? (see Zechariah 9:9) What should the religious authorities have understood?

continued »

5 Why, then, do they reject Jesus? (see Mark 12:24, 38–40)

6 How will you treat Jesus if "you do not know the Scriptures or the power of God?"

Your questions on this HOME STUDY

WEEK 6
JESUS - HIS RESURRECTION

> *Discuss any questions arising from last week's HOME STUDY.*

> *Look together at Mark 12:1–11 and answer the questions below:*

1 Who is the "man" in Mark 12:1 and "the owner" in Mark 12:9?

2 What do we learn about God from Mark 12:1–2?

3 How do the tenants treat the owner in Mark 12:3–5?

4 What do we learn about God from Mark 12:3–5?

5 What does the owner do in Mark 12:6? Who does this remind you of?

6 How do the tenants treat the son? (see Mark 12:7–8)

7 What do they expect the outcome of their actions will be? (see Mark 12:7–8)

8 What is the owner's response? (see Mark 12:9)

9 Do you think the tenants would have behaved as they did if they believed that the owner would judge them?

10 In Mark 12:10–11, Jesus quotes Psalm 118, applying the quote to himself. What is "marvellous" about Jesus being rejected?

"He has risen! ... just as he told you." (Mark 16:6–7)

- Three days after Jesus' death and burial, Mark records how the women who had watched Jesus die go to the tomb to anoint the corpse.

- They experience three shocks of escalating intensity:

  - the huge stone had been "rolled away" from the tomb's entrance

  - instead of Jesus' body, they saw "a young man dressed in a white robe" in the tomb

  - the young man told them: "He has risen!"

- The Gospels alone tell us of eleven different instances when Jesus was seen after his death – at different times, in different places to different people. He ate with them, talked with them and walked with them, just as he did before his death. In 1 Corinthians 15:6 we read that five hundred people saw Jesus at one time.

- "For he [God] has set a day when he will judge the world with justice by the man he has appointed. He has given proof of this to all men by raising him [Jesus] from the dead" (Acts 17:31). The resurrection proves that Jesus will "judge the world." It also warns us that after death people will be raised to face judgement.

- The resurrection is a great hope, because it proves that there will be eternal life for those who put their trust in what Christ did at the cross. Everything that Jesus has promised will come to pass... "just as he told you."

NOTES

WEEK 6

- "Heaven is not a pipe dream, or a cruel mirage, but an amazing reality earned for us by Christ's death, and proved by Christ's resurrection." Has this changed your view of heaven?

- "For God has set a day when he will judge the world with justice by the man he has appointed. He has given proof of this to all men by raising him from the dead" (Acts 17:31). What's your reaction to this?

- Do you believe the resurrection is possible?

HOME STUDY

> *Read Mark 14:1 – 16:8.*

Summary: Jesus goes willingly to his death on the cross and so fulfills God's purposes.

> *Use the following study to help you explore the passage. There's room at the end for you to write down any questions you'd like to discuss next time.*

1 How do we know that Jesus' death was not a mistake or accident? (see Mark 14:12–31, 48–49, 61–62)

2 Even though Jesus knew it was his mission to die, was death easy for Jesus? (see Mark 14:33–36; 15:34)

3 What does his death accomplish? (see Mark 15:38)

4 Although the disciples understand who Jesus is, they still haven't grasped why he has to die. What does this passage say about how people will respond if they understand who Jesus is, but not why he had to die? (see Mark 14:50, 66–71; 16:8)

continued »

5 Who *does* see and understand? (see Mark 15:39)
   Why is that surprising?

6 Jesus' resurrection demonstrates his power over death.
   What answer do you have to the inevitability of death?

Your questions on this **HOME STUDY**

> *Congratulations! You've now finished reading Mark's Gospel.*

EXPLORING
CHRISTIAN LIFE

**You'll cover this section on a weekend or day away.
It's an opportunity to explore and ask questions about the church,
the Holy Spirit, prayer and the Bible. It's also a great opportunity
to get to know people in your group a bit better.**

EXPLORING CHRISTIAN LIFE
THE CHURCH

TALK OUTLINE

"He who walks with the wise grows wise, but a companion of fools suffers harm." (Proverbs 13:20)

- The Christian life can be very hard, so it is important for Christians to remember that they have been chosen by God (1 Peter 1:1–2) and that they have "a living hope": the certain hope of heaven (1 Peter 1:3).

- When the Bible talks about "the church," it is simply referring to all those people who have put their trust in Jesus.

- Peter tells Christians they should "love one another deeply, from the heart" (1 Peter 1:22). Without this mutual support that the church family provides, it will be hard to persevere.

- Christians should build around them a team of wise people who will help them to follow Christ until they reach heaven.

NOTES

GROUP DISCUSSION

- **"He who walks with the wise grows wise, but a companion of fools suffers harm" (Proverbs 13:20). Do you think this is true in your own experience?**

- **"...love one another deeply, from the heart" (1 Peter 1:22). Do you think this is realistic?**

THE HOLY SPIRIT

"It is for your good that I am going away. Unless I go away, the Counsellor will not come to you; but if I go, I will send him to you." **(John 16:7)**

- The Holy Spirit ("the Counsellor") who comes to live in Christians is the Spirit of Christ himself.

- The Holy Spirit's work has many aspects. For example, he:
  - makes people aware of their sin
  - changes Christians from within by giving them the desire to please God
  - gives each Christian gifts to be used in the service of other Christians
  - brings peace that comes from being in relationship with God

NOTES

EXPLORING CHRISTIAN LIFE

- "I had no inner peace." What is it that makes people feel like this?

- Having explored Jesus' life, how would you feel about his Spirit coming to live "with you" and "in you" (John 14:17)?

PRAYER

TALK OUTLINE

"Trust in him at all times, O people; pour out your hearts to him, for God is our refuge." (Psalm 62:8)

- Christians pray in order to deepen their relationship with God.

- Jesus teaches his followers to address God as "Our Father." A Christian's relationship with God is a privileged, intimate one.

- When Christians pray, they are praying to the "Sovereign Lord" who is in complete control of everything that may happen.

NOTES

EXPLORING CHRISTIAN LIFE

GROUP DISCUSSION

- **Do *you* ever pray?**

- **God is "the Sovereign Lord, who is in complete control of everything that may happen to you." How might this affect your life?**

THE BIBLE

"All Scripture is God-breathed." (2 Timothy 3:16)

- The Bible contains all kinds of writing – history, poetry, prophecy, songs, biography – but whatever the style, the underlying message is the same: how we can be rescued from our sin.

- Reading the Bible enables Christians to know God.

- The Christian's "delight is in the law of the LORD, and on his law he meditates day and night" (Psalm 1:2). The Bible shapes the thinking of Christian people.

- "He is like a tree planted by streams of water" (Psalm 1:3). The Christian is refreshed and replenished by reading the Bible.

- "Mary has chosen what is better" (Luke 10:42). Christians must choose to make time to read God's word, no matter how busy their lives become.

NOTES

GROUP DISCUSSION

- **"Mary has chosen what is better" (Luke 10:42). What choices do *you* need to make to hear God's word?**

- **The person who delights in God's word is "like a tree planted by streams of water, which yields its fruit in season" (Psalm 1:3). Do you think the Bible could play this role in your life?**

WEEK 7
WHAT IS A CHRISTIAN?

> Discuss any questions arising from last week's HOME STUDY.

> Look together at Mark 14:1–11 and answer the questions below:

1 How do the different people in this passage respond to Jesus?

	RESPONSE TO JESUS
The religious leaders	
"Some of those present"	
The woman	
Judas	

2 How does Jesus respond to what the woman does for him? Why? (see Mark 14:6–8)

3 Would Jesus have been surprised at the plotting of the religious leaders?

4 Would Jesus have been surprised at Judas' scheme?

5 What does Mark 14:9 tell us about Jesus?

6 So how should *we* respond to Jesus?

"If anyone would come after me, he must deny himself and take up his cross and follow me." (Mark 8:34)

- In Mark chapter 8, we see that Jesus' disciples have begun to recognize who he is. Peter identifies Jesus as "the Christ," that is, the King promised in the Old Testament who would have the power and authority of God himself.

- Jesus then teaches them that he has come to die. He knows that the only way sinful people can be brought back into a relationship with God is by dying in their place.

- Then Jesus says, "If anyone would come after me, he must deny himself and take up his cross and follow me."

  - Denying self means no longer living for ourselves but for Jesus.

  - Taking up our cross means being prepared to follow him, whatever the cost.

- Jesus gives a convincing reason to live like this: "What good is it for a man to gain the whole world, yet forfeit his soul?" (Mark 8:36).

WEEK 7

- **"What good is it for a man to gain the whole world, yet forfeit his soul?" (Mark 8:36). How would *you* answer that question?**

- **Jesus said: "If anyone would come after me, he must deny himself and take up his cross and follow me" (Mark 8:34). Do you feel you could do this?**

- **"A Christian is someone who is prepared to follow Christ, whatever the cost." What is the cost?**

If you've become convinced of who Jesus is and what he came to do, and you understand what it will mean to follow him, you might like to pray the following prayer:

Heavenly Father, I have rebelled against you. I have sinned in my thoughts, my words and my actions – sometimes unconsciously, sometimes deliberately. I am sorry for the way I have lived and ask you to forgive me. Thank you that Jesus died on the cross so that I could be forgiven. Thank you that I can now see clearly who Jesus is and why he came. Please send your Holy Spirit to help me follow him whatever the cost. Amen.

HOME STUDY

> *Read Ephesians 2:1–22. Next week, you'll look at a part of this chapter with your group.*

WEEK 8
CONTINUING AS
A CHRISTIAN

> Look together at Ephesians 2:1–10 and answer the questions below:

1 How does Paul describe human beings in Ephesians 2:1–3?

2 How is the Christian described in Ephesians 2:4–10?

3 What is it that makes the difference between the person described in verses 1–3 and the person described in verses 4–10? (see Ephesians 2:4–5)

4 In what way does salvation come to us from God? (see Ephesians 2:8)

5 What is the appropriate response to God's grace? (see Ephesians 2:9–10)

6 What can you contribute to your salvation?

"Jesus said, 'It is finished.' " (John 19:30)

- Christians will face opposition: from the world around them, from their own sinful nature, and also from the devil, who wants to undermine the Christian's relationship with God.

NOTES

- There are certain things Christians can be sure of in the face of opposition:

  - the presence of the Holy Spirit, who gives Christians the desire and the strength to overcome this opposition.

  - the promises of God in the Bible that provide assurance of God's love and sovereign power.

  - Christ died to pay for sin past, present and future. "There is now no condemnation for those who are in Christ Jesus" (Romans 8:1).

- As he died, Jesus said, "It is finished." No matter how hard life gets, these words remind Christians that their sin is paid for, they're at peace with God and destined to be with him in heaven.

WEEK 8

GROUP DISCUSSION 2

- **Do you feel able to trust God's promises in the Bible?**

- **Can you see how Jesus' words – "It is finished" (John 19:30) – might affect your life?**

HOME STUDY

> *Re-read Mark 3:1 – 4:41. Next week, you'll look at a part of these chapters with your group.*

WEEK 9
CHOICES - KING HEROD

> Look together at Mark 4:3–20 then answer the questions below:

1 After telling the parable in verses 3–8, Jesus interprets it in verses 13–20. So, what does the "seed" represent?

2 What are the four possible outcomes when God's word is preached? (see Mark 4:15–20)

3 What does it mean if the hearer has "no root"?
(see Mark 4:17)

4 How do the "worries of this life, the deceitfulness of wealth
and the desires for other things" choke the word?

5 How have *you* responded to hearing God's word?

"The king was greatly distressed, but because of his oaths and his dinner guests, he did not want to refuse her." (Mark 6:26)

- King Herod was deliberately rebelling against God.

- John the Baptist, a man Herod knew was "righteous and holy," repeatedly warned him to stop rebelling. But Herod would not turn away from what he knew was wrong – he would not repent.

- Finally, on Herod's birthday, "the opportune time came." His wife asked for John the Baptist's head on a platter. Herod had a choice: he could either repent, or give her what she wanted. Under pressure from his wife, his friends and his dinner guests, Herod once again chose not to repent.

- Later in life, Herod meets Jesus. "He plied him with many questions, but Jesus gave him no answer" (Luke 23:9). Rejecting Jesus' call to repent and believe may earn us the approval of other people, but it will eventually earn us the rejection of Jesus.

NOTES

WEEK 9

GROUP DISCUSSION 2

- **Why do you think Herod refused to repent?**

- **John's preaching greatly disturbed Herod. How does Jesus'
teaching make you feel?**

HOME STUDY

> *Look back through your notes and jot down any questions you still have,
> so that you can discuss them in the final session next week.*

WEEK 10
CHOICES - JAMES, JOHN & BARTIMAEUS

GROUP DISCUSSION 1

> Use the time to ask any questions you still have.

TALK OUTLINE

"'What do you want me to do for you?' Jesus asked." (Mark 10:36 and 51)

- James and John ask Jesus for power and prestige. So Jesus knows that they cannot have understood what it means to follow him. He corrects their thinking by reminding them that even he "did not come to be served, but to serve, and to give his life as a ransom for many" (Mark 10:45).

- If you've already put your trust in Jesus, you may need to learn what James and John learned: following Jesus is about service, not status.

- Bartimaeus asks for mercy. Jesus heals him. He immediately begins to follow Jesus.

- If you haven't yet put your trust in Jesus, you need to do what Bartimaeus did: cry out to him for mercy and follow him.

NOTES

GROUP DISCUSSION 2

- **Who do you identify with most: James and John or Bartimaeus?**

- **What choices will *you* make based on what you've learned during *Christianity Explored?***

- **"If you could ask God one question, and you knew it would be answered, what would it be?" How did you answer that back in Week 1? How would you answer it now?**

Thank you for making time to attend *Christianity Explored*. If you've become convinced of who Jesus is and what he came to do, and you understand what it will mean to follow him, you might like to pray the following prayer:

Heavenly Father, I have rebelled against you. I have sinned in my thoughts, my words and my actions – sometimes unconsciously, sometimes deliberately. I am sorry for the way I have lived and ask you to forgive me. Thank you that Jesus died on the cross so that I could be forgiven. Thank you that I can now see clearly who Jesus is and why he came. Please send your Holy Spirit to help me follow him whatever the cost. Amen.